PICTURES FROM THE SURFACE OF THE EARTH

Photographs by Wim Wenders

Wim Wenders, photographed by Donata Wenders, 2000

PICTURES FROM THE SURFACE OF THE EARTH

PHOTOGRAPHS BY WIM WENDERS

SCHIRMER ART BOOKS

My special thanks for the production of the prints for this exhibition and the print reproductions for this catalogue go to Michel Karman and Chip Levitt in Los Angeles as well as to Volker Leppers and Dagmar Mietke in Düsseldorf. I would likewise like to offer Heiner Bastian my heartfelt thanks for his friendship and advice, to In-Ah Lee and Marla Ulrich for their unflagging efforts and last but by no means least to my wife Donata, without whom neither the exhibition nor this catalogue would exist.

Wim Wenders

The book *Pictures from the Surface of the Earth* is based on an exhibition at Deutsches Centrum für Photographie attached to the Nationalgalerie and the Kunstbibliothek der Staatlichen Museen zu Berlin in the "Hamburger Bahnhof – Museum für Gegenwart", 2001. We would like to thank Heiner Bastian, Eugen Blume, Nicole Hartje, In-Ah Lee, Doris Rector, Lothar Schirmer, Maria Ulrich and in particular Wim Wenders for making the exhibition possible. We would also like to cordially thank the Association of Friends of the Nationalgalerie for their generous financial support.

Peter-Klaus Schuster

ANGLES

Wim Wenders' cities and deserts at the end of photography

Peter-Klaus Schuster

7

BETWEEN HEAVEN AND HOME

Photographs by Wim Wenders

Nicole Hartje

13

PLACES

Wim Wenders

18

PLATES

21

LIST OF PLATES

with notes by Wim Wenders

110

ANGLES
Wim Wenders' cities and deserts at the end of photography

I. Humboldt and the surface of Berlin

Eduard Gaertner's painting *Panorama vom Dach der Friedrichswerder-schen Kirche*, made in 1834 (ill. 1), is one of the most invaluable pictorial and educational testaments to Berlin. Like the angel in Wim Wenders' film *Wings of Desire*, Schinkel, Beuth and Alexander von Humboldt look down over the new city of Berlin from their vantage point high above the confusion of houses in the immense city around 1830 as if they were its guardian angels. Gaertner's panorama, which was to initiate the thirst for photographic vistas, and in fact already benefits from such a wish, already intimates the ongoing transformation of Berlin during the 19th century, in the course of which the metropolis became a seemingly endless cityscape. Under the sign of industrialization, the rapidly expanding large cities became ossified deserts, the sea of houses spreading out beyond the reach of even the broadest angle of vision. The attempt to offer a simultaneous grasp of the whole progresses from the painted panoramas and photography to film and its unlimited camera pans.

It is especially interesting that in his panorama Gaertner places not only Schinkel and Beuth, the leading architect and pioneering social econo-mist, but also Alexander von Humboldt a viewer of this early process of the city seizing hold of the countryside. There could certainly have been no more knowledgeable an observer of the urbanization of the earth's surface, the initial transformation of European cities into unmistakable deserts populated with houses and the occasional cultural oasis, than Alexander von Humboldt. Starting from Berlin he traveled first to London and then to Paris as the epitome of urban density before departing to explore the surface of the earth in South and Central America, including Cuba; after his long-postponed return from Paris to Berlin, he subsequently set out on another protracted exploration that took him deep into Siberia. In his own lifetime, as the scholarly world traveler that he was, Alexander von Humboldt's contribution to our knowledge of the earth's surface by way of positivistic observations, indexing and description of all perceptible natural occurrences was considered a true marvel. Over and above his lectures at the university, in the form of his "Cosmos" lectures at the Sing Academy, Alexander von Humboldt ensured that the broader general public also became acquainted with his knowledge of the world – and it included, following his meeting with Daguerre in Paris, a resolute belief in the future of photography. This is probably why, in Gaertner's painting, we see Humboldt, as the probably greatest authority of the day on the earth's

Ill. 1: Eduard Gaertner, *Panorama von Berlin vom Dach der Friedrichswerder-schen Kirche*, 1834

widely different surfaces, standing on the lookout platform of Schinkel's church; in other words, he is positioned in front of the buildings embodying public scholarship, namely the university and the library.

Ever since Alexander von Humboldt had climbed Chimborazo he had thus become the legendary seer of the world from above; and Gaertner places him high above Berlin and as its politically liberal and enlightened world conscience; in conversation with others, he looks out at Berlin's in all its superficial appearance. It is no coincidence that Gaertner places children full of interest on the church's roof alongside Humboldt who, with his cosmopolitan curiosity, is immersed here in local details. In this way, Gaertner already illustrates the notion of a "childhood treasure trove" – a word Wim Wenders uses to describe the elementary field of visual experiences such as is acquired in childhood and on the basis of which the adult then sees and experiences the world for the rest of his or her life. The children are the innocent eyes whose unprejudiced interest still really sees.

Gaertner, whose anti-academic and essentially industry-informed career took him from porcelain to panorama painter, via Berlin, Paris and Moscow, and had had him most recently again ornament pretty Biedermeier perspectives, had emerged as the major architectural painter between Schinkel and Menzel. And in Gaertner we have the tangible example of a painter of pictures programmatically dedicated to bourgeois well-being and fully familiar with the technical achievements of the photography of the day, a man who visualized urban life in Berlin as the palimpsest of the many possible histories of an assiduously observed surface. With Alexander von Humboldt, Schinkel and Beuth, this realistic view from above out over the city's beautiful facades and backyards still has something of the utopian perspective of the good fortune of bourgeois society about it, its diligence, its cultural and technological achievements. Gaertner's panoramas of Berlin are painted educational vistas and deliberately constructed political landscapes.

II. End of photography

By contrast, Wim Wenders' photographs of the earth's surface as collected here stand at the other end of European perceptual history, as it were. Indeed, Wenders' old panorama camera is itself now a fossil when compared with the reality of the modern image media. The latter has emerged as the opposite of the former panoramic desire for vision. Whereas in the past an almost hypertrophic effort was made to place any number of realities next to one another, in the hope that this would offer a higher-powered knowledge of the world, the development of video technology has led to the quasi-democratic erosion of almost all subject matter, however remote it may be. Thanks to ultra-modern digital image processing technologies, perception now has the ability to visually manipulate reality in all conceivable ways. "Each individual pixel," or so Wim Wenders claims, "every one of the smallest pictorial units, each 'pictorial atom' can be changed. Since there is no longer an original, there is also no longer any proof for 'truth'. In the final instance, the digital electronic image will make the divide between 'reality' and 'second-hand reality' deeper than ever before, perhaps rendering it insurmountable. In other words, pictures have completely changed their being in the course of time, have been transformed from unique painted works into digital clones. The latter have arisen with incredible rapidity and have multiplied at a similar speed. We are being bombarded by images to an extent unprecedented in human history" (p. 119).*

The age of technical reproducibility has thus entered a completely new dimension. Unlike paintings, there is no longer that one, unique original that can be copied countless times. And, as with photography and then film, there is no longer only an original, the negative, that does not exist if not copied. With the advent of electronic images, and soon with digital images, the age of the technical revolution, or so Wim Wenders suggests, will transcend itself – and will score a complete triumph, for now "there is no negative any longer, and likewise no positive, even the idea of an original is pointless. Everything is a copy. Any distinction is arbitrary" (p. 104).

III. Cities and deserts

In light of such arbitrariness, the maker of images regains his dignity, among other things, by dint of consciously returning to the outdated technique of photography. Moreover, according to Wim Wenders, image producers must also possess that sensitivity to restlessness, that wish to travel "to the end of the world" – as his film title would have it. Life as a road movie through homelessness, as a permanent "departure for the unknown" (p. 59), leads to the status of a nomad, for whom all places are foreign and who therefore has a heightened vision. Wim Wenders, as a passionate urbanite – "I'm crazy about cities" – recognized during each set of travels prior to making a new film that he was fascinated by the opposite image, namely the desert: "I must say that I now almost just as much like empty landscapes, such as deserts, and then it is probably fair to talk of two antipodes, where something arises between them and where cityscapes truly sometimes border on desertscapes" (p. 64).

In 1991, in a lecture he held before an audience of Japanese architects, Wim Wenders again brought up this idea of the antithesis of city and desert. Both areas no longer border on each other, but mingle and thus comment on each other: "I love the city! But sometimes you have to leave it. To view it from the distance to find out what it is about it that you love. I am familiar with the Us and Australian desertscapes. Now and again, in a desert you come across a residue of civilization: a house, a former road, an old railway line or even a deserted filling station or motel. In a way, these are the opposite of the experiences you make on entering a free space in the midst of a city. No-man's land within a city places the surrounding surfeit of the city in perspective, causes it to appear in a different light, and the sudden appearance of the relics and remnants of civilization make the surrounding desert all the emptier" (p. 126f.).

The "pictures from the surface of the earth" which Wim Wenders brings together in the present volume all emphasize precisely this visual experience. Owing to the omnipotence of global civilization, in the photos of Wim Wenders, as Nicole Hartje has described in detail, the cities become emptied deserts, and the deserts abandoned suburbs of this civilization of isolation. While in the days of Gaertner's panoramas, at the beginning of industrialization, cities spread out with optimistic vitality into the surrounding nature, in Wim Wenders' pictures nature fights back. The desert stands once more at the end of urban civilization. Everything becomes transformed into grandiose empty desertscapes, from which humans have more or less retreated and in which nature has once again gained the upper hand over civilization. These are pictures devoid of human beings, in which the signs of

civilization that have been left behind, its traffic signs, ads (complete with the promises these contain), all tell of the people who were once here. These, the photographs of a restless traveler on the surface of the earth at the end of urban civilization, are at the same time a contribution to the archaeology of the absence of humans on the surface of the earth. In these new city deserts, only the children playing constitute a hopeful sign of some joy in life – on the part of an almost extinct or solitary species.

IV. Angles

Wim Wenders is of the conviction that it is the stance of the photographer, his "angle", which defines the photo. This awareness of the subjective component is Wenders' response to the increasing loss of reality in photographic images under the sign of their digitalization. If the photo is no longer the only reliable guarantor of reality, as it was once thought to be and as so many artists feared, then all the more importance must be assigned to the insight into the photographer's subjective "angle".

What Wim Wenders has said on the "angle" of film – in a conversation that has gone on for years on the "truth of images" – also holds true for his attitude toward photography. Here, "angle" means nothing other than the morality and respect the image-maker has for what exists before his recording apparatus: "You try as far as possible to respect what is there and to preserve the substantive truth of what it is you convey. Perhaps not everyone will readily believe me, but I maintain that in each angle in a film you can see the angle of those who are behind it and are responsible for it. I believe that each angle in a film reflects the angle of the filmmaker. And in the final instance, in each angle you can see what was in front of the camera and also always what is behind the camera. For me, a camera is something which functions in both directions. It shows both its object and the angle of those who are responsible for it. This is a fantastic process in the case of filmmaking" (p. 87).

It is therefore hardly surprising that in his "Lecture on Germany" in 1991 Wim Wenders again focused on this elementary perceptual problems of the "angle". The German language, or so Wenders, who describes himself as a cosmopolitan, claimed, had remained "his language". It followed from this that "my language was also my stance, my relationship to the world, my 'angle'. (The German word 'Einstellung' is a marvelously precise word for a filmmaker and can hardly be adequately rendered in another language. After all, shooting from a specific angle or taking an angle on things – the one is not possible without the other)" (p. 191). It bears remembering that Wim Wenders had since childhood, or thanks to his childhood, progressed a long way toward becoming an American. All those imported friends he had so enjoyed since childhood, the US comic strips, the US films and the US music, all had one thing in common: they were fun, offering a feeling of the great wide world compared with the confined straightjacket of Germany. Wenders considered Mickey Mouse and Mark Twain the real "school of life": "Huckleberry Finn's Mississippi was closer for me than the Rhine or the Mosel" (p. 193).

Wenders considers it obvious that such childhood impressions were important as something that shaped his overall angle on life: "I believe that today we all know that a person is largely formed during childhood and that the treasure trove of dreams and sensibilities largely originates in childhood. And almost everyone I know who writes, paints or makes music draws on this trove" (p. 59). The fact that these "childhood treasures" from the Promised Land of America then became a nightmare for Wim Wenders has to do with the commercial exploitation of images from that dream frontier: "John Ford's landscapes are now 'Marlboro Country', the American dream an ongoing ad campaign. I 'returned home', among other things because I couldn't stand life in Disneyland, because I no longer felt the breath of 'true images', and only the bad breath of mendacious images" (p. 194).

If, in global civilization, all that exist are pictures of pictures, if in this world of global reproduction even cities exist in duplicate, such as Paris or Odessa, the one in Europe the other in Texas, if entire countries such as Germany or Japan, or so Wenders suggests, are decidedly "absorbed by foreign images and stories" (p. 195), "if the world of images comes completely unstuck", then to his mind what remains is the certainty of another culture – "the counter-culture in which nothing has changed and in which nothing will change, that of story-telling, of writing and reading, the *word* " (p. 197).

With a pathos reminiscent of Hölderlin, Wim Wenders recommends that the salvation for Germany – where, unlike the United States, pictures can no longer forge identity and where images "are discredited once and for all" (p. 197) – must be to retreat into language, to rely on the word as all that perseveres and redeems. "Our salvation", he continues apologetically, "and some of the words have to be dug out from under piles of rubble, our salvation in this country, and how unholy it is at present, is our language. It is differentiated, exact, subtle, endearing, sharp-edged and caring all at once. It is rich. It is the only rich asset we have in this, our country that considers itself rich but is not. It is all that the country no longer is, has not yet become again, and will perhaps never become again" (p. 198).

V. Images as history

The illness from which images suffer, their loss of reality, their inflationary surfeit – all this can be healed, Wim Wenders suggests, by "story-telling, by the word" (p. 76). Anyone who makes pictures from an angle that references them to the level of words, narration and history, guides them back into the subjective domain and thus into renewed sincerity: "I have learned from past mistakes: the only protection against the danger or illness of a self-satisfied image is belief in the primacy of history. I have learned that each image possesses only one level of sincerity in relation to a figure within history" (p. 121).

This is an astonishing confession by an image-maker, namely that images can only be saved from the glut and commercialization of pictures if "they tell a story" (p. 121). Yet, to Wenders' mind the opposite also applies, namely that all stories latently brag, while all images contain sincerity, as seeing is perception: "In other words, I believe that truth is latently possible in the act of seeing" (p. 60). After all, observing perception as telling the story of an image is already an approximate version of the truth. In this act of immersion-in-the-world by dint of seeing we can sense the links to the art of Caspar David Friedrich, something Wim Wenders has not denied. "In many of his pictures, Caspar David Friedrich also shows the act of seeing, or he shows how we see. In your work there are many references to how seeing functions, or how we see. Windows are opened, repeatedly someone is looking out of a window. What is actually so great about seeing?" (p. 59)

Ill. 2: Caspar David Friedrich, *Der Mönch am Meer*, 1808/10

Ill. 3: Edward Hopper, *Early Sunday Morning*, 1930

Wim Wender answered Peter W. Jansen's question in a manner that is just as applicable to Friedrich's *Mönch am Meer* (ill. 2) and its unlimited panoramic sweep (as if my eyelids had been cut off – is how Heinrich von Kleist described seeing the painting) as it is to Wenders' own panorama pictures: "For me, seeing is an immersion in the world, and thinking is always a process of gaining distance from it" (p. 60).

Pictures acquire the quality of the sincere not only by the angle they clearly take on the history of seeing, on perception, for example by some panorama-like extension of the picture to create some manifest immersion in the world. Not only the history of seeing, but also the (hi)stories of life provide angles that enable us to reflect on the images with their suggestive nature and thus render them sincere again. The canon of such fascinating pictures that wish, as pictures, to tell stories which former art student Wenders has established for himself includes the paintings of Edward Hopper. Wenders believes that in the domain of painting Hopper epitomizes the production of pictures that aspire to connect a wish to see and a wish to narrate. In his paintings of urban settings, Hopper, so Wenders suggests, "always starts from a specific location, even where his pictures sometimes seem highly abstract and universal. There's the famous picture of a street in New York, with the barber's shop in the middle (ill. 3). I believe that is a highly exciting picture in the way it references photography and film. I have often seen that picture […] It's a picture where you expect that the very next moment something will happen and it will change – perhaps the

lighting. It is a picture waiting to pounce […] Edward Hopper's paintings are also the beginnings of stories. A car is just pulling in to the gas station he paints and someone is sitting behind the wheel who has just been shot in the stomach. These are always the beginnings of American movies" (p. 171).

Given that he so praises this quality of wishing to tell stories in Hopper's oeuvre, it is hardly surprising that in his photographs Wim Wenders often takes his cue from Hopper's pictorial world, devoid as it is of humans. Many of Wenders' most impressive photos seem to transform or continue Hopper's paintings, in an urban present through the medium of photography, whereby the angle chosen ensures that the picture can tell many different stories. Given this reverence for Hopper's pictorial world, and Wenders succeeds at times in linking it to the aesthetically laconic tone of David Hockney's paintings, it is not surprising that Wim Wenders also holds the photographic oeuvre of Walker Evans and Robert Frank in such high regard – both men produced work so closely related to Hopper's paintings. For example, just as Walker Evans discovered writing as a pictorial element, so, too, his photographs provide pictorial beginnings for many-layered stories. Wim Wenders constructs his photos of America, almost all of which feature writing, in the same vein – as an epilogue to the American myth, written in a visual idiom. The pictures of the surface of the earth thus become the representation of the world as a book full of inscriptions, from which we can glean the widest variety of stories and, at times, truths – all depending on the angle we take. The titles of his photo books, *Written in the West* or *Once. Pictures and Stories*, attest to Wim Wenders' fundamental conviction that the picture has a literary and narrative structure as the visual location of one or many possible stories.

VI. Epilogue – looking back at Berlin

The salvation of pictures by the stories which are generated by the angles of the pictures, be they stories of subjective seeing or the visible beginnings of unsolvably complex stories behind the pictures – it was against the foil of this pictorial poetics that Wim Wenders experienced the moment when the Berlin Wall came down, in 1989, while in the Australian desert: "Out there in the desert there was of course no TV and I therefore saw not a single picture from Berlin. What remained were phone calls via satellite, and it was very difficult to get a line, and a few photos that were faxed through, completely inadequate in terms of their quality. I didn't learn more. Everything took place in my imagination, as it were […] The experience was quite different, far more introspective by virtue of the fact that out there the entire flood of pictures that washed over Germany, where everyone saw the images thousands of times over, simply did not exist. I had to paint it all before my inner eye. Or perhaps I should say, I was lucky enough to […]" (p. 185).

At the end of photography it was always the inner eye of the image-maker that caused the clearer image of the unique history of a city and its highly vivid surface to appear in the empty desert. It is this inner angle taken by the photographer which imbues the pictures with their truth. This stance, or so Wim Wenders believes, applies to film, photography – and the viewers. At the same time, Wim Wenders also follows Humboldt in thinking that only if you have seen the distant close up on the surface of the earth will you also see what is close at hand, even from a distance.

Peter-Klaus Schuster

All page numbers refer to Wim Wenders, *The Act of Seeing*
(Frankfurt/Main, 1992, published in English by Faber & Faber)

BETWEEN HEAVEN AND HOME
Photographs by Wim Wenders

I. Pictorial stories

Wim Wenders' stories always start with pictures. With pictures of places, towns, landscapes or streets. Just as many of his films unravel not in terms of a script but a travel route, so the exhibition "Pictures from the Surface of the Earth" actually consists of a trip across almost twenty years through towns and landscapes in Germany, the United States and Havana, through forests and temples in Japan, along the coast of the Sea of Galilee and countless times along the seemingly endless roads through the Australian outback. Only seldom do we encounter photographs of people and faces.

What we see are the objects found by a photographer and in the choice of subject matter, section and moment they reveal his feel for the mythology of places, for their simple facticity and on occasion allow for insightful links back to his films. For the first time, the exhibition "Pictures from the Surface of the Earth" brings together photographs relating to all Wenders' different works and to places, starting with "Written in the West", the first exhibition held at Centre Georges Pompidou in 1986, through the "Wim Wenders – Photos" show organized by the Goethe Institute and presented worldwide, to the shots that he took in 1998 in Havana while filming *Buena Vista Social Club*. Pride of place goes to eighteen panorama views, which, like no other photographic medium, capture the breadth of the landscape, giving the bizarre natural formations an unusual perspective. While the circumstances under which they arose may have been highly varied, these pictures share the myth of the lonely traveler, a myth which repeatedly reminds us of the transience of all being.

II. From Paris, Texas, via Coober Pedy, South Australia to Havana – Wim Wenders' landscape photographs

Wenders' photographic journey commenced in 1983, when he spent several months criss-crossing the Midwest scouting for the right loca-

tions for *Paris, Texas* and used photography as a means of sharpening his sense of light and landscape. He photographed the long since abandoned lounge of a motel, a drive-in, deserted gas stations, the front of a supermarket, and a phalanx of trucks no longer in service. With the astonished eye of a European and his camera, a Makina Plaubel at that time, he recorded for posterity railroad tracks that disappear in a straight line into nothingness, signposts that have long since lost their referent and shops that have long since been abandoned. The photographs exude calmness and balance, astonishment in the face of the breadth and beauty of a landscape that has lost nothing of its appeal and is stronger than civilization – present in the pictures as fleeting garish traces.

Wim Wenders' photographs always take the surface of a landscape, a city or a street as their starting point. When asked how he finds his subject matters, Wenders narrates that he does not search for them, but that they reveal themselves to his eye by dint of their color, form and material being – the structure of their surfaces – before he has even found the final, real location he seeks. This was what happened when he arrived in the deserted town of Las Vegas in New Mexico, where in the afternoon sun he found himself captivated by an empty store called "Entire Family". Butte, in Montana, burnt out and dilapidated by an ongoing recession and unemployment, brought to his mind images of Poisonville, that city in Dashiell Hammett's *Red Harvest* and led to him making a series of photographs. Only few of his images so clearly manifest the decay and gradual disappearance of a city such as do *Square with Cut-Out Figures in Butte, Montana* in which hardly a house remains standing and it is left to the power lines to remind us of the once flourishing township.

With his photographs from the Midwest Wenders takes up that mythically charged notion of landscape already alluded to in the title "Written in the West". They refer like almost no other series he has produced to that theme of US identity that is less a geographical term and more a symbol, the former lodestar for the settlement of the country. In this way, Wim Wenders' photographs continue the tradition of earlier series, such as Walker Evans' "American Photographs" (1938), Robert Frank's "The Americans" (1958) and finally Robert Adams "The New West" (1974) – which painted a comprehensive portrait of the landscape and US society, bonding a pictorial representation with moral thrust. The United States of the day was reflected in the light of the American dream – that beacon of new beginnings and optimism. This notion of the West as a sphere that was actually new is still intimated by Wenders' photos, but immediately undermined by the details. For example, here we only see a few isolated individuals, people who have long since fled these regions, leaving the testaments to their civilization, their apartments, cinemas, stores and streets, including the billboards and neon lights, to decay. In Wenders' photographs it is hard to escape the impression that civilization admittedly reached these regions and left its mark, but that nature has long since seized hold of the landscape again.

Symbolic of the evident fall of these towns is the presence of the billboards and signs that Wenders so stressed in his early photographs. The signs are inevitably on weathered housefronts, abandoned cinemas or bars – and their message therefore reaches no one. Their frequency means that they predominate in the ambient structure of a form of anonymous communication that has completely lost its voice. All that is left are street signs, signposts and assertions, but never a person addressed who could understand these positions and make use of them. While back in the 1930s Walker Evans was able to highlight the variety of ad signs in the town and country as a cultural asset, as expressions of life and energy, in Wenders' work they have deteriorated into some apocalyptic semiotic chaos. Now, all that are left are signals, but no context.

For his early photographs, with but a few exceptions, Wenders chose a frontal perspective. Only seen frontally could the object be extricated from its surroundings and lent the theatrical status typical of the loneliness of the US badlands. Only thanks to an untrammeled gaze do the buildings preserve their neutrality and identity, eliding any explicit angle and reference to the person of the photographer. For all the central perspective which Wenders adopts vis-a-vis the weathered entrances

and obsolete signs he nevertheless manages to sensitively structure the picture. In the photo, existing objects, house facades, wall panels or a large-size sign chart the course of the section chosen, emphasize the deliberate linearity, differentiate and cause the panoply of manmade colors and forms to contrast with the return of nature. A key structural element here is the line of the horizon, which bisects the picture into two equal halves and in the middle of which he has always placed the motif: a cross, a mountain peak, a sign – pivots to which all the other elements in the picture refer.

Among the landscape photographs it is those of Australia that most incisively document the fascination and occasionally the humbleness which overcome Wim Wenders as a European when confronted by the overwhelming breadth of this country. Since his first trip to Australia, in 1977, he has repeatedly traveled there bearing a panorama camera, initially with a Russian 35mm camera, then later with a Japanese Art Panorama, a medium-sized camera allowing him to take shots with a higher resolution and exceptional depth with 17:6 plates. Sized almost two meters by over four meters, these most recent landscapes almost exceed our ability to grasp them with our eyes. Comparable with earlier works, these photographs with their extraordinary dimensions attest to Wenders' art of composing pictures deliberately and with a strong feel for the proportions. While in *Street Front in Butte, Montana* and *Junk Yard, Coober Pedy, South Australia*, the horizontal extension is visually underscored by the a road or fence running parallel to the lower edge, in *On the Golan Heights* Wenders makes use of vertical ascendant lines which are at loggerheads with the expanse of the breadth. He skillfully captures the soft horizontal undulations of the mild hills in *At the Horizon: The Rocky Mountains* and thus emphasizes their motion. Even if unintentional, these photographs can without a doubt be equated with the monumental mode of the panoramic vistas that were so popular in the 19th century. They tend, like the classical panoramas before them, to compel the eye to move horizontally, to meander across the individual elements in the landscape.

Among the various possible techniques available, Wenders chose the panorama camera and thus a means of not only reproducing the limitlessness of this landscape, its sublime nature and silence, its truly endless horizon and blinding light in grandiose manner, but even enhancing this effect. In the case of the photos from Australia, photographs taken from a great height that cause the landscape to become a moving ocean alternate with shots taken at eye height and in which a corrugated iron fence or a scrapyard denote civilization and its decay. As previously with "Written in the West", this photographic "road movie" now at most shows traces of human life, and even they seem to have been taken over by nature. In a special way, this landscape embodies the destiny of so central importance in the way the young nation of Australia sees itself. In these panorama photographs, nature appears as the yardstick which none of the documents of human presence can match. The photographs are at times a melancholy hymn to freedom and a world that, at the foot of Ayers Rock, seems to blend with a different world.

In 1998, accompanied by renowned slide guitarist Ry Cooder, Wenders traveled to Havana, immersing himself in the initially alien but fascinating world of Cuban culture and its music – in order to shoot his documentary *Buena Vista Social Club*. Unlike *Paris, Texas*, where he had photographed each location prior to the filming, the pictures of Havana and the Cuban countryside have little to do with the film and are far more independent in character. Detached from some filmic context, the subject matter develops a sensuous magic and beauty of its own, attesting to the mood as created by the music, the picturesque colors, and the quite manifest decay of Havana as a city. With the exception of the photo of the small boy entitled *Boy at Bat*, whose gaze and swing may be directed at a future that bears greater hope than the present, these photographs also evoke a feeling of passing and decay. They speak of the yearning for a past that imbues the present with its tragic, morbid beauty.

Unlike the photographs of Australia, here Wenders used the panorama camera primarily to record the architecture, portraying the narrow houses by use of imperious portrait formats, while the very next moment the focus seems to shift and to pan across the street in its entire length, tarrying in the distance. If we take subjects such as the American limousine rolling past and the boy playing baseball, then Wenders would appear here to have used the technique to intimate movement and thus approximated filmic techniques in order to lend photography a narrative element without thus limiting its range.

Wenders discovers stories in all these landscapes. Be it the man with the cowboy hat, who apparently is heading straight into the abandoned AA office, the flower-adorned grave of a Native American in Montana or the almost illegible writing on a rock in Japan, Wenders evidently firmly believes in the narrative power of landscapes. "There are landscapes which truly exude stories. They conjure up their stories, in fact they really create them." By means of photography, he hopes to detect these stores and bring them to life. To Wenders' mind, not only props, such as a billboard, a car, a cigarette pack or a chair, are fragments of a story – for the landscapes are the main protagonists.

III. "Each photo is a reminder of mortality." –
Photographs as objects of transience.

For Wenders, a central element when photographing is the experience of time. Independent of the place where he happens to be at a particular moment, be it an abandoned town in the Midwest, somewhere in the Australian outback, in the thicket of a Japanese bamboo jungle or on Alexanderplatz in Berlin in the midst of fog, photographs always reminds him of the uniqueness of each moment. "Each photo remembers our mortality. Each photo deals with life and death," Wenders wrote in *Once*, his album of photos and stories. Only a few photos convey so clearly the transience as does a shot of dusk or of an immense scrapyard in Australia. Wenders says that precisely such "surfaces" of the earth attract him in particular, those places that kindle the wish in him to seize hold of the images with his eyes and preserve them.

Wender is driven by passion like any collector. It would appear to be a passion for the present but it is in fact always coupled with a sense of the past. His enthusiasm for a subject does not relate primarily to its contents or meaning, but instead hinges on simply confirming its existence, its uniqueness, irrespective of which qualities make it appear unique. Wenders, too, dedicates himself to rendering reality antiquated by photographing it, and he makes each of his photographs an antique. Each photo can then be compared with the Romantic genre of creating pictures of ruins, an artificial ruin that emphasizes its historical character and is intended to imbue nature with a special appeal, namely the appeal of the past. The open character of Wenders' photographs confirms that everything passes. The arbitrary status of the photographic statement alludes to the fact that in the final analysis reality cannot be classified and can only be grasped as the sum of incidental fragments. In the past, we find an expression of dissatisfaction with reality in the yearning for a different world. In modern society this is expressed in the desire to reproduce and capture this world.

IV. Film director Wim Wenders as photographer

Wim Wenders is one of the most successful film directors of his generation and, at the same time, a photographer. Tracing the relation between his silent and his moving pictures could mean discovering a causal relationship in the assumed linear progression from photography to film. While each photo conveys the impression of the past, the individual film frame seems to grasp the struggle between time and the image of the future. The filmic image is an illusion of the present, the photographic counterpart offers the certainty of the past.

In Wenders' oeuvre, the relationship of photography and film is, however, far more complex. Neither of the two media is all-excluding: instead they supplement and benefit each other. For example, a piece of photographic journalism by Walker Evans was the starting point for Wenders' film *Kings of the Road* (1976). During the Great Depression, Evans was commissioned by the Farm Security Administration to travel the Southern states and compile a series of photographs that would impressively document the impact of the economic disaster. When Wenders then started filming *Kings of the Road* in the border area between East and West Germany, often when selecting a location he took his cue from Evans' photographs. "It was often the case that we stopped on the road to film a scene because a section of the countryside or an architectural motif reminded us of one of his photos." *Paris, Texas* (1983) and, later, *To the End of the World* (1991) are both based on a series of photographs or are directly connected with the experiences he has made with photography, architecture, the landscape, color and light in the future film location. For Wenders, photography often means the first step to a film, cautiously sounding out a location. Quite apart from the possibility of photographically devising a film, the latter is often affected by the photographic experiences. Thus, in all his films we find allusions to his preference for pictures that burst the limits of a particular story: In *The Goalkeeper's Anxiety at the Penalty Kick* (1971)

it is the close-up of an apple on a tree, in *Alice in the Cities* (1973) an auto dealer who is interested more in the Polaroid shot of the hero than in the car and in *The State of Things* (1981) there is a striking shot of an Isetta parked before the empty expanse of beach on the Atlantic coast.

There have been any number of photographing filmmakers. Yet none of them has blended film and photography to the extent achieved by Wim Wenders, who is keenly aware of the specific potential of the two media. While in film the landscape usually forms the backdrop to the figures, photography makes up for this by presenting the long shot as the essence. Unlike the close-ups against an out-of-focus background so prevalent in film, Wenders feels that specifically photographs offer a broad scope for the imagination, because the resolution and depth allow even the smallest of details to be identified. For Wenders, photographing is in the final instance "an act in time, during which something is torn from its time and instilled with a different kind of duration." Only photography offers him a means of capturing the image and preserving it: "Compared with film, photography has something final about it."

Nicole Hartje

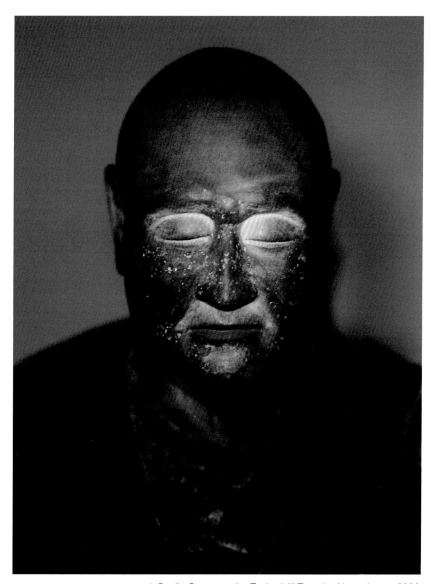

1 Ganjin Statue at the Toshodaiji Temple, Nara, Japan, 2000

PLACES

There are places I remember all my life
Though some have changed...
All these places had their moments...
In my life I've loved them all. (Lennon/McCartney)

Places where we spend our lives.
Places that we visit for just a moment.
Places we discover by chance.
Places that attract us by their name on a map alone.
Places we will never see again.
Places we can never forget.

Places we long to come back to.
Places that scare us.
Places that comfort us.
Places that make us feel at home.
Places we find repulsive.
Places that fill us with awe.

Places we dreamed about
before we ever got there.
Places we got lost in
and places that we lost.

Places condition us.
Places protect us.
Places destroy us.

As metaphorical as they might appear,
places are always real.
You can walk around in them
or lie down on the ground.
You can take a stone with you
or a handful of sand.
But you can't take the place with you.

You can never really own a place.
Even the camera can't.
And if we take its picture,
we're only borrowing the place's appearance
for a little while,
nothing but its outer skin, its surface.

Some of the places I photographed
are about to disappear,
might already have vanished from the surface of the Earth.
They will only survive in photographs,
or better: The memory of them
will have to cling to the pictures we have of them.

Other places will outlive us
and even our efforts to capture them on photographs.
More so: They will survive any trace of us.

In a million years,
when no one will be around any more
to even remember us faintly,
some of these places will.
Places have memories.
They remember everything.
It's engraved in stone.
It's deeper than the deepest waters.
Their memories are like sand dunes,
wandering on and on.

I guess that's why I take pictures of places:
I don't want to take them for granted.
I want to urge them
not to forget us.

Wim Wenders, Los Angeles, August 2001

2 Bamboo Forest, Nara, Japan, 2000

3 Rock with Inscriptions, Nara, Japan, 2000

4 Inside the Toshodaiji Temple, Nara, Japan, 2000

5 Praying Mantis, Nara, Japan, 2000

6 Toshodaiji Monastery, Nara, Japan, 2000

7 Mossy Ground, Nara, Japan, 2000

10 "Safeway", Corpus Christi, Texas, 1983

8 Street Front in Butte, Montana, 2000

9 "Blue Range", Butte, Montana, 2000

13 Lounge Painting # 2, Gila Bend, Arizona, 1983

11 Square with Cut-Out Figures in Butte, Montana, 2000

12 "Entire Family", Las Vegas, New Mexico, 1983

16 Used Book Store in Butte, Montana, 2000

15 Lounge Painting # 1, Gila Bend, Arizona, 1983

14 AA Centre in Paris, Texas, 2001

17 Evening near Santa Fe, New Mexico, 1983

18 Indian Cemetery in Montana, 2000

19 At the Horizon: The Rocky Mountains, Montana, 2000

20 "Entrance", Houston, Texas, 1983

22 Two Cars and a Woman Waiting, Houston, Texas, 1983

21 Dust Road in West Australia, 1988

23 Joshua and John (behind), Odessa, Texas, 1983

24 Junk Yard, Coober Pedy, South Australia, 1988

25 Wall in Paris, Texas, 2001

26 "The Valley of the Winds", Northern Territory, 1988

27 The "Bungle Bungles", West Australia, 1988

28 "Lizard Rock", South Australia, 1988

29 Beetle Cemetery, Coober Pedy, South Australia, 1988

30 In Omote-Sando, Tokyo, 2000

31 Dusk in the "Bungle Bungles", West Australia, 1988

32 After a "Tote Hosen" Concert at the Westfalen Stadium, Dortmund, 2001

33 Meteorite Crater, West Australia, 1988

34 "Scheunenviertel", Berlin, 1992

36 On Alexanderplatz, Berlin, 1992

35 "The Field of Blood", Jerusalem, 2000

37 Jerusalem Seen from Mount Zion, 2000

39 Jerusalem Seen from the Mount of Olives, 2000

38 The Road to Emmaus, near Jerusalem, 2000

41 On the Adriatic Coast, 1994

40 Lake Galilee before Sunrise, 2000

42 Beach Front in Tel Aviv, 2000

43 On the Golan Heights, 2000

44 Boy at Bat, Havana, 1998

45 The Pink Building, Havana, 1998

47 Shoe Shine Stand, Havana, 1998

46 Local Store, Havana, 1998

48 Havana from across the Bay, 1998

49 The Orange Building, Havana, 1998

50 The Black Car, Havana, 1998

1 Ganjin Statue at the Toshodaiji Temple,
Nara, Japan, 2000, 86.4 x 66 cm

"Ganjin" was the monk
who brought Zen Buddhism over to Japan
from the Chinese mainland,
and taught the Emperor and his family.
He founded the Toshodaiji Monastery
in the eighth century,

1,200 years ago.
Ganjin was blind.
This small statue was made by his disciples,
shortly before his death.
Its face was not depicting a man with closed eyes,
but, indeed, a blind man!

2 Bamboo Forest, Nara, Japan, 2000
380 x 143.5 cm

Dozens of mosquitoes
were descending on me
while I tried to hold my camera still.
I just hoped
they wouldn't land on the lens.

3 Rock with Inscriptions, Nara, Japan, 2000
178 x 203.5 cm

I did not put the red leaf there.
I don't know
what the inscription says.
I found the rock
in the thicket
of one of the gardens
of the Toshodaiji Temple.

4 Inside the Toshodaiji Temple,
   Nara, Japan, 2000, 180 x 132 cm

I did take a picture
of the small temple
and the urn under its roof,
behind this wall.
But what moved me
was the mossy surface
of the gray stone,
on the outside.

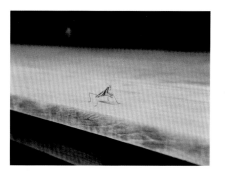

5 Praying Mantis, Nara, Japan, 2000
   124 x 155 cm

I had never seen
such a big insect in my life.
Its name seemed ironic,
given that the Praying Mantis was sitting
on the front porch
of the central building
of the Toshodaiji Temple.

6 Toshodaiji Monastery, Nara, Japan,
   2000, 114 x 239 cm

The monks who lived here,
centuries ago,
had each occupied the space
of two tatami mats.

7 Mossy Ground, Nara, Japan, 2000
   124 x 145 cm

In the parks
of the Toshodaiji Temple,
there were hidden clearings,
covered with the softest moss.
I took my shoes off
to walk on it.

8   Street Front in Butte, Montana, 2000
    178 x 447 cm

Early morning,
not a soul on the streets of Butte, Montana.
It was as if I had walked into my favorite painting
of Edward Hopper:
"Early Sunday Morning", painted in 1930.
It was Sunday, indeed.

9   "Blue Range", Butte, Montana, 2000
    125 x 152 cm

I found out later
that this building had once been a brothel.
A red light district
to really get the blues …

10 "Safeway", Corpus Christi, Texas, 1983
    178 x 210 cm

A few moments ago,
someone probably stood on the yellow step
in front of that door,
smoked a cigarette,
flipped the butt into the hot street
and went back to work inside.
Behind the wall and its promise
of a safe way,
it was certainly nice and cool.

11 Square with Cut-Out Figures in Butte, Montana, 2000
    178 x 447 cm

I walked around a corner
in downtown Butte,
and there they were, those black cut-outs,
hanging around the square like phantoms,
the shadows of the missing people
from those colorful lounge chairs
I had photographed years earlier
in Gila Bend, Arizona.
Around the next corner I found the "Haunted Hotel",
and in the local bookstore that night
plenty of "Montana Ghost Stories".

12 "Entire Family", Las Vegas, New Mexico, 1983, 178 x 210 cm

Houses have faces
and characters,
like people.
This one, with the wrinkles on its forehead,
made me laugh and feel sad
at the same time.

13 Lounge Painting # 2, Gila Bend, Arizona, 1983, 125 x 145 cm

I don't know
how long it's been
since anyone has sat down
on those chairs.
They didn't seem to miss people much.
They were involved
in deep conversation
amongst themselves.

14 AA-Zentrum in Paris, Texas, 2001, 160 x 125 cm

I never saw his face.
The man unlocked the door
to the local AA center in Paris, Texas.
I had lost sight of Travis eighteen years ago,
but for a split second,
I thought it was him.

15 Lounge Painting # 1, Gila Bend, Arizona, 1983, 125 x 152 cm

It took me hours to find somebody
who could open up the lobby
of the old "Stout's" hotel on Main Street in
*   Gila Bend.*
It had been closed for years already.
That painting over the Coke machine haunts
*   me ever since.*
It's the dream version
of the perfect beginning
of a road movie.

16 Used Book Store in Butte, Montana, 2000
124 x 234 cm

I was somehow reminded of Truffaut's "Fahrenheit 461"
on my Sunday morning stroll through Butte.
In Bradbury's science fiction novel
"used books" would have been a contradiction in terms,
and would only have been available
in stores like this one.

17 Evening near Santa Fe, New Mexico, 1983
125 x 145 cm

All day long
I had wanted to photograph
one of those hills
with the little dark bushes.
At dusk,
when I had given up on my desire,
I found the one
I had been looking for.

18 Indian Cemetery In Montana, 2000
178 x 447 cm

The wooden church next to the Indian Cemetery
was all boarded up.
I walked around for an hour
and read all the names on the graves.
Some of the men had died in the Vietnam War.
Traveling Wolf had died before.
According to the cross on his grave
he was 22 years old
when Edward Curtis photographed the Blackfeet Indians
in this part of Montana, in the year 1900.

19 At the Horizon: The Rocky Mountains, Montana, 2000
178 x 447 cm

Summers are short in Montana
and the sky bigger than anywhere else.
Those hay rolls looked like pawns
in a giant chess game.
The nearest town was called "Choteau".

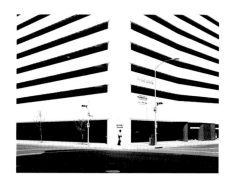

20 "Entrance", Houston, Texas, 1983
124 x 150 cm

Why do so many parking structures
look so ugly,
if they can look so perfect, too?

21 Dust Road in West Australia, 1988
178 x 447 cm

I remember the name of the deserted farm
this dust road was leading to:
"Gordon Downs".
There was a tennis court in the overgrown garden,
and it was still fenced.
Birch trees were growing out of its red clay,
and birds were nesting on the umpire's chair.

22 Two Cars and a Woman Waiting,
Houston, Texas, 1983, 124 x 150 cm

This was from inside out
of the beautiful parking structure
in Houston, Texas.
The woman was standing there in the heat,
waiting for the light to turn green,
when the two cars drove up.
Edward Hopper was a movie buff,
as I learned from his biography,
and I bet he's seen some of the early
Hitchcocks …

23 Joshua and John (behind), Odessa, Texas,
1983, 125 x 170 cm

I can guess
how the wives
of the drivers
of the busses
of the Calgary Baptist Church
in Odessa, Texas,
called their husbands
when they came home from work.

24 Junk Yard, Coober Pedy, South Australia, 1988
178 x 447 cm

It is so hot in Coober Pedy
that most people live underground,
under those sandy mounts.
I stayed at the "Dug-Out Motel".
The main building material here is corrugated iron.
No other surface, I feel, lends itself so well to photography.

25 Wall in Paris, Texas,
    2001, 160 x 125 cm

If I had had a hammer,
I would have tried
to chip off more from that stucco
and uncover the entire precious fresco
underneath.
But I only had a camera.

26 "The Valley of the Winds", Northern Territory, 1988
178 x 447 cm

This place is formed by a group of monoliths
called "The Olgas".
Today, you can't walk into the "Valley of the Winds" anymore.
It was declared a sacred site of the Aborigines.
They recognize mythical beings in these mountains
from the beginning of time.
They are right.

27 The "Bungle Bungles", West Australia, 1988
178 x 447 cm

The "Bungle Bungles" are an ancient coral reef.
Millions of years ago,
this part of West Australia
was covered by the ocean,
when it was still "Gondwanaland".

28 "Lizard Rock", South Australia, 1988
   178 x 447 cm

We had slept on the sandy ground,
rolling out one of those mattresses
that the Australians call "swags".
The flies woke us up early in the morning,
with the first ray of sunlight touching the high grass.
The night before, when we had chosen this place as a camp,
I hadn't noticed the nearby mountain.
I was out of my sleeping bag in a second,
to take this picture in my underwear.

29 Beetle Cemetery, Coober Pedy, South Australia, 1988
   178 x 447 cm

This car cemetery
was on the outskirts of Coober Pedy,
a mining town in South Australia
with the biggest opal fields in the world.
These "Beetles"
were gems, too, in my book.

30 In Omote-Sando, Tokyo, 2000
   124 x 150 cm

The "Comme des Garçons" store front
had changed a lot since I had last seen it.
A space-ship had landed,
with T-shirts for sale.

31 Dusk in the "Bungle Bungles", West Australia,
   1988, 178 x 447 cm

We put up camp here for one night.
For six weeks
I slept with nothing but the stars above me,
the Southern Cross.
When we returned to the cities,
I could only sleep on balconies for a while.

32 After a Concert by "Die Toten Hosen" at
   the Westfalen Stadium, Dortmund, 2001
   124 x 152 cm

With all that loud music still ringing in my ears,
the shouts and the hammering
of the roadies disassembling the stage
seemed muted,
like an eerie silence,
forever the soundtrack to this picture.

34 The Old Jewish Quarter, Berlin, 1992
   124 x 160 cm

The sign says:
"So what?
It's not as bad as it looks."

33 Meteorite Crater, West Australia, 1988
   178 x 447 cm

I discovered this place on a map of Western Australia, years ago.
It was just marked with a circular sign saying
"Meteorite Crater".
I never made it there by car.
It would have taken a day or two
to reach it on the desert road
that leads past it, west of Alice Springs.
On a location survey with a small airplane, years later,
I asked the pilot to fly the detour.
He circled the enormous crater,
then landed on the dust strip next to it.
In the midday heat, I walked for an hour
into the middle of the giant circle.
I didn't take a picture there.
Seen from inside, the crater was invisible.

35 "The Field of Blood", Jerusalem, 2000
   178 x 447 cm

The gospel according to Matthew reads:
"Judas realized that Jesus was doomed.
Overcome by remorse,
he gave back the 30 silver coins to the high priests, saying:
'I've sinned. I've betrayed an innocent man'.
They said: 'What do we care? That's your problem'.
Judas threw the silver coins into the Temple and left.
Then he went out and hung himself.
The high priest picked up the silver pieces,
but then didn't know what to do with them …
They decided to get rid of it by buying the 'Potter's Field'
and use it as a burial place for the homeless.
That's how the field got called 'Murder Meadow',
*A name that has stuck to this day." ***
Other translations call it "The Field of Blood".
When I finally located the place,
south of the old city of Jerusalem,
it seemed like the most haunted grounds
I had ever walked on.
Even the birds avoided it.

36 On Alexanderplatz, Berlin, 1992
   124 x 170 cm

That was
when most of the Russian soldiers
had already left the former East Germany.
These looked so lost
in time.
Can you feel
how scratchy those coats are?

* Scripture taken from *THE MESSAGE*. Copyright © 1993, 1994, 1995.
  Used by permission of NavPress Publishing Group.

38 The Road to Emmaus, near Jerusalem,
2000, 178 x 447 cm

On the third day
after Jesus was crucified,
two of his disciples
walked sadly to the village of Emmaus,
about seven miles out of Jerusalem,
when they were joined by a stranger ...
I found traces of the old Roman road.
It was getting dark
when we arrived in Emmaus.

37 Jerusalem Seen from Mount Zion,
2000, 290 x 115.6 cm

According to the Holy Scriptures,
those Jews who have the privilege
of being buried on Mount Zion
are the first ones to rise from the dead
on Resurrection Day.
If that happened in our times,
they would have to bear facing
*   the El-Aktza Mosque*
on the Temple Mount.

39 Jerusalem Seen from
the Mount of Olives,
2000, 290 x 115.6 cm

Jesus often retreated
to the Mount of Olives
or spent the night there.
It is still a silent place today.
And there are still olive trees.

40 Lake Galilee before Sunrise, 2000
178 x 447 cm

Every now and then a fish jumped up.
Birds were flying by in the far distance.
Nothing had changed, it seemed,
on Lake Galilee,
since Jesus had stopped here one morning,
two thousand years ago,
and said to two fishermen throwing out their nets:
"Come with me.
I will make a new kind of fisherman out of you…"
According to Matthew,
"They didn't ask questions,
but simply dropped their nets and followed."

41 On the Adriatic Coast, 1994
124 x 165 cm

It was off-season.
The Seventh Seal
was playing all alone.

42 Beach Front in Tel Aviv, 2000
124 x 145 cm

I stood transfixed
by the blue neon light
and the purple sky.
It was hot and humid,
and I wish I remembered the music
that came blaring
out of those speakers.

43 On the Golan Heights, 2000
178 x 447 cm

Raymond Chandler once wrote:
"There's nothing emptier than an empty swimming pool."
But a skiing resort in the summer
can be just as vacant.

44 Boy at Bat, Havana, 1998
   100 x 239 cm

The two of them
played with a piece of wood for a bat,
and a ball made out of rags.
They were very serious about baseball.
All Cubans are.
They are the most elegant players.

45 The Pink Building, Havana,
   1998, 244 x 95 cm

Electricity is always a problem in
   Havana.
Refrigerators don't work all the time,
and neither do door bells nor telephones.
Nor elevators, of course.
Pulling things up outside of the houses
seemed like a more reliable solution.

46 Local Store, Havana, 1998
   100 x 239 cm

You couldn't buy much in the groceries,
neither in Havana, nor in the country shops
on the other side of the bay.
Food was difficult to find, especially vegetables.
On the other hand: I never saw a beggar.
Back in Los Angeles, it was a shock
to remember how much there was to buy everywhere.
And how many beggars stood in the streets
and opened their hands.

47 Shoe Shine Stand, Havana, 1998
   244 x 95 cm

Shortly before I took the picture of the
   shoe-shine stand
underneath the arch of this glorious building,
I had walked into an old movie theater in
   the neighborhood
called "America".
On the mosaic floor of the entrance lobby,
it showed a big, simplified map of the
   Americas,
laid out in colored and golden stones,
with a little black bean
lying smack dab in the middle
between North and South America,
like in a womb:
That was Cuba.
And the shoe-shine stand,
when I came back out into the sun,
was American, too, I thought.
In the true sense of the word.

48 Havana from across the Bay, 1998
    100 x 239 cm

Taking the tunnel under the river
and coming out on the other side,
you were in a different world.
Havana was an apparition
out of the future
of its own past.

49 The Orange Building, Havana, 1998
    244 x 95 cm

Some colors were reoccurring
all the time in Havana.
The explanation I was given
for all those cars
of the same light blue was
that a couple of years ago
blue had been the only paint available.
There had been green or yellow years as well.

50 The Black Car, Havana, 1998
    100 x 239 cm

I waited a long time for a car to come by
that I liked.
Sometimes you need such help
in order to know
when to press the button.

The essays by Peter-Klaus Schuster and Nicole Hartje were translated from the German by Jeremy Gaines.

Schirmer Art Books is an imprint of
Schirmer/Mosel Verlag GmbH, Munich.
For trade information please contact:
Schirmer Art Books, John Rule, 40 Voltaire Rd.,
London SW4 6DH, England or
Schirmer/Mosel Verlag, P. O. Box 22 13 41, D-80506 München
Fax: 089/33 86 95

Lithography by NovaConcept, Berlin
Design by Klaus E. Göltz, Halle
Printed and bound by EBS, Verona

ISBN 3-8296-0011-9
A Schirmer/Mosel Production
www.schirmer-mosel.com